# Renditions

Also by Reginald Gibbons

<u>Poetry</u>

*Roofs Voices Roads*

*The Ruined Motel*

*Saints*

*Maybe It Was So*

*Sparrow: New and Selected Poems*

*Homage to Longshot O'Leary*

*It's Time*

*Creatures of a Day*

*Slow Trains Overhead: Chicago Poems and Stories*

*Last Lake*

<u>Fiction</u>

*Sweetbitter*

*Five Pears or Peaches*

*An Orchard in the Street*

<u>Translations</u>

*Selected Poems of Luis Cernuda*

*Sophocles, Selected Poems: Odes and Fragments*

*Euripides, Bakkhai (with Charles Segal)*

*Sophocles, Antigone (with Charles Segal)*

*Guillén on Guillén: The Poetry and the Poet (with Anthony L. Geist)*

<u>Criticism</u>

*How Poems Think*

# Renditions

## Reginald Gibbons

Four Way Books

Tribeca

For Josephine and Benjamin

Library of Congress Cataloging-in-Publication Data

Names: Gibbons, Reginald, author.
Title: Renditions / Reginald Gibbons.
Description: [New York] : [Four Way Books], [2021] |Identifiers: LCCN 2020037834 |
ISBN 9781945588730 (trade paperback)
Subjects: LCGFT: Poetry.
Classification: LCC PS3557.I1392 R46 2021 | DDC 811/.54--dc23
LC record available at https://lccn.loc.gov/2020037834

This book is manufactured in the United States of America and printed on
acid-free paper.

Four Way Books is a not-for-profit literary press. We are grateful for the assistance
we receive from individual donors, public arts agencies, and private foundations.

This publication is made possible with public funds from the
New York State Council on the Arts, a state agency.

PROUD MEMBER

[clmp]

We are a proud member of the Community of Literary Magazines and Presses.

Contents

ONE

TWO

THREE

SOURCES

# O N E

*Make up your mind, Crab!*
*You're half inside your house, half*
*inside my own, now!*

—after Richard Wright

Swear—

—by the cold beards
        of frosted stones,
by stoic stead-
        fast winter pines,
by the crystal-
        frosted window
where my lonely
        candle peers out:
*swear*: when summer
        comes I won't let
even one skiff
        pass by on my
river without
        my inviting
it: Stop! Moor here!
        I won't let one
singer stand at
        my listening
door without my
        saying—Come in!
Let us hear you.

*—after Marina Tsvetaeva (1919)*

3

# Honeycombs and Cobwebs

Heaviness and tenderness—they're sisters
the same way bees and wasps will ply
the same sweet languid rose.

                        Sands cool. People die.
Yesterday's sun is borne away in a hearse.

Heavy honeycombs and tender webs!
It would be easier to lift a boulder than to speak
*Your* name.
          But there's still one hope—a golden
mirage: to throw time off my weary back.

The air that fills my lungs flows dark. And time's
ploughed under. Roses rise from the humble earth.
Whirling slowly, these roses—tender, heavy—
plait rose *tristesse, tendresse,* in a double wreath.

                          *–Osip Mandelshtam (1913)*

## Anemone


The anemone stares with
its wide-open petals
at all the new morning
flowers around it.


~


Awake through half the night as
you sleep, I'd happily go

sleepless for a century
if I could do it

here, listening to the air slowly
swaying inside the room, and beyond

the window, too, like calm sea waves
among these boats we call our

houses. Both the air and I are
trying not to wake you, and so's

the hermit thrush that's singing
now as softly as it can.

~

Even one anemone's
a cosmos. Maybe the stars
were made only for
laughing—with their
inconceivably bright
breath.
          Add everything up—
orchard, fence, pond, wild
wooded mountains, and in
the empty kitchen a glass
of clean water and the whole
pitch-black universe, lit by
frothing nebula-
white screams . . .
                    All of it at once,

all of it
is what one child, soft-
stemmed as a thin weed,
still unable
to comprehend her own suffering,
has in her own small

heart and does not
know how to let
pour out.


−*after Boris Pasternak (1917)*

# Boy, Hiding

To rest, hidden, mid-afternoon, lightheaded and hot
in the only shade—inside the hollow center of a big yaupon,
where the glare needled in and no one else would come—
and to listen for wasp wings, to watch for copperheads

or rattlers, to study the red ants in a spread-out horde
searching heat-cracked ground around you, many ant
miles from the great city mounds you've dynamited
with hoarded firecrackers, and they've rebuilt.

To peer out of the sheltering bush at the low flat roof
of our house, its crushed white gypsum repelling the sun
while the locusts—we called them—raised their buzzing
to a screech across the bare acres . . . Self-exiled from

the house, on hands and knees crawling out, with empty
water jar, back into your heat-stroke exurb of Houston,
and wondering if all life, all labor of grown men, wouldn't
require hiding somewhere from the scald of anger—like inside
a tall bush topped with a throbbing paper nest of hornets.

*—after Eugenio Montale (1922)*

8

# Paris . . . Moscow, 1925

*[Marina Tsvetaeva addressing Boris Pasternak]*

Versts, miles—such distances
        and dys-stances—
you and I so sundered by them—
        disposed
at two extremes. We failed not
        to become,
each of us, a world apart
        from the other.

Time strides on roads of time,
        refugee
days straggle their way here
        and can't go
back because what was, where
        they began—
where you are—is no longer,
        while where I am,
no place will be made for me
        by these maimed years.

~

I've said farewell to the fields
        of Russian rye—

where a woman may need to
                    shield her eyes
from fires of wood and blood, from
                    graves, rivers,
imprisoned outstretched arms . . .
                    from any
alloy of tendons and visions. . . .
                    I am your
detached retinue. You're mine.

Gusts of rain splatter against
                    my glass heart
like happiness or misery.
                    I—still here
at my bodily outpost—
                    in this city
of resplendent indifference,
                    penury,
a feral winter in the soul.

~

You—distant but visible in
                    the *soviet* of

poetry—which you hate! You—not
              inside their stanzas
of ordure, murder, evils. Be
              like Homer inside
his hexameters, instead. Chant
              your sunset
quatrains and reach toward me—
              reach—like a train
slowly crossing the steppe—
              here. Where my
one hand—for lack of the best rhyme:
              the word that loves
its discovered mate-word—is
              holding the other.

*–after Marina Tsvetaeva (1925)*

# The God Eros, Who Cannot Be Thwarted

overpowers not just

        and unjust human beings

only, but animals

        too—and even the breath of

gods trembles, shakes, stops, bursts,

        when Eros wings into them,

even from far away,

        at their culmination. Great

Zeus Himself retreats some-

        times from the overthrowing

comeliness of mortal

        bodies. He Himself is far

too weak—even He!—to

        ward off Eros. Even He

wants, more than anything,

        anything, just to give in.

*—Sophocles (5th century BCE)*

# One Leaf, Two Leaves

The faintest sound—
the fingertip of a leaf touching
the windowpane, or a tiny
spring trickling over pebbles,
or droplets of light rain
      on the forehead of my childhood . . .

The lightest caress—
bare feet in summer on a soft dirt path,
a hand that attempts for the first time
      desire's touch,
or the clean darkness lying light
      as a bedsheet over one's sleepless self. . .

A nameless fervor within me
so often doesn't seem to be
      mine yet is me.

Nearly everything near or far
that reaches toward me soothes
me and wounds me. You—

your presence, even though it's
not my life, is my life.
The way two unnoticed leaves can be
proof of the world's breath.

*−Luis Cernuda (1931)*

# But What Does He Do?

One afternoon it comes to him that his arms are
no better than clouds—
it's not possible to hold the body
you desire, or hold onto the hopes
you had.  Not possible not to let go.

Fate can go bed-checking
the summer-sky constellations with an astral
clipboard in its hand,
but here what he needs
is arms at least
as strong as the wind from the sea.
And a kiss as immersing as the sea.

But what does he do? With his
inherited lips all he does is speak
words: words to the ceiling,
words to the floor,
words to his scribbled page on which
he's crossed them all out.
And as he angles, drifting,
under his own low sky, he can see right
through his reaching
cloud arms, his cloud hands.

*–Luis Cernuda (1929)*

# But A Guy Goes By

A guy goes by with a long loaf of bread on his human shoulder.
And after that I'm going to write about my doppelgänger?

In the alley, I see a girl looking for meat scraps and orange rinds.
Is now when I'm supposed to write about the Infinite?

Another guy, sitting on the curb, scratches himself, nabs a louse
in his armpit, smashes it. And we're going to chat about psychoanalysis?

A homeless woman's sidewalk-sleeping—her foot's behind her back!
And I'm going to meet a friend so we can talk about Picasso?

Some other guy, swinging a stick at my bones, has invaded my body.
So then, later, at the doctor's, I'm going to talk about investments?

This crippled dude goes wobbling by with a big kid, arm in arm.
And after that—what? I'm going to read the art reviews?

Someone is shuddering in the dark. Coughing, spitting blood.
When exactly would it be appropriate to theorize the Inner Self?

A roofer falls, he dies, and from now on he goes without lunch.
So now I'm going to invent some flashy new poetic effects?

This diamonds-bought-and-sold guy—he uses rigged scale weights.
So . . . make sure everybody at the opera sees that you're weeping?

Too near my building, this skinny guy deals heroin laced with fentanyl.
Is this really the time to take alien sperm and astral travel seriously?

The old couple at a funeral, crying as they walk holding hands—
and what's the protocol when you're voted into the Academy?

Sitting at the kitchen table, somebody's lovingly cleaning his handgun.
What exactly is the good of talking about where we go after we die?

A girl's run over by a local Nazi aiming his station wagon at her.
And we have to hear about "very nice people on both sides" and not scream?

A neighborhood granny goes by counting something on her fingers.
And the biggies are saying we must make sure the banks are OK?

*—after César Vallejo (1937)*

# Elegy: Green We Love You Green


*Verde que te quiero verde* even when

dying can yet be, can yet become, a green


plenitude—the jade the pine the fern the mint.

We can breathe the green breath of your lines, green shade


may somehow fade bereavement away, while in

your words live the sixty shades of green that words


can see, words that bleed green, words that your pen-nib

dance-drags in green dust under the olive trees,


as you throw song-notes at their silver-green leaves

and end your stanzas with green razor blades—


your *verde* so clack-heeled, your swarms of midnight

*palmas* clapped with such exuberance of green

anguish and joy, your vowels so green in guitar-
light *rasgueados*—in leaf-thrashing wind-lashed

frenzy, *frenesí*, to hear again that your
voice cannot not matter . . . *¿No ves la herida*

*que tengo*—he imagines a knife-wound from
his chest to his throat—*desde el pecho a la*

*garganta?* Now he stands one finite instant
from the bullets, with his betrayed companion—

a teacher, also to be murdered—and two
more. Now the uncanny presence of the scent

of basil and the word's green sound: *albahaca*
*(al-habáqah)* . . . We so need a billion dawn

hours—*albas*—of love. But I'm no longer I

*pero yo ya no soy yo* nor is this house

any longer my house *ni mi casa es*

*ya mi casa.* We so want him to have lived.

His house, his piano—unbetrayed, not deceived . . .

But he was nilled and annulled so long ago.

*Verde que te quiero verde* we still chant

in *la nada que no y la nada que sí.*

*—for Federico del Sagrado Corazón de Jesús García Lorca (1898-1936)*

## Back to the Village

It's dark when we arrive at the doorway
where I spoke my long-ago goodbye
as the rooster was singing one of his epics.
The door's locked. I call out
and there's no answer.

The stone bench beside the door
where Mamá brought my big brother
into this bright world so he would saddle
backs for me. But I would later ride them bare,
rambling through narrow streets and out
beyond—village boy that I was.
This very bench of stone is where I left
my hard childhood to yellow in the sun.
And this doorway framed by grief?

God, in His peace . . . somewhere else—
far from this place! My horse, mere beast,
snorts—he too is calling to them. He's scented
something, he clops his hooves on the cobblestones,
he snorts. But he's not sure—
he swivels his pricked ears.

Papá must still be up. Praying. Maybe
even now he's still fretting: Something's made
this boy late. My simple-hearted sisters—
incessantly whispering their busy
little fantasies to each other, getting ready
for a holy day that's not coming.
And almost everything
has been prepared. I hope and wait.
My heart's an egg that almost . . .
but something's blocking it,
something's in the way.

That big family we forsook not so
long ago—this night nobody's still
awake, nobody's put even one candle on the altar
so that we'd come back—my soul and I.

I call out again. And . . . nothing.
I and my soul both hush. We begin to weep.
The animal snorts, tosses his head, whinnies.

But for all eternity they're all asleep.
Yet this is so much for the best that at last
my tired horse, standing beside me, shakes

his head, softly jiggling his bridle and the reins.
But he falls asleep, then he wakes, he bows
his head low, this night,
he falls asleep again. And every time he wakes,
he nods to me and he says—
It's all right. Everything's all right.

—César Vallejo (1922)

# On the Continent's Far Edge

Walking in cold rain along the top of the high cliffs.
Caught in a remote coastal town three slow days—
roads are washed out. In the old wooden hotel,
we wake to more rain. I read in Spanish, sleep in English.

Vapor. At the edge of the cliffs we can hear
the sodden ground below us loosening, huge
clumps slopping onto the beach—wet earth-words
spoken in the language of Earth. Old cliff-top

railway tracks, still nailed to rotting ties, and bent,
rusted, torqued over time, twisted—greatest
of dragon-snakes still slow-writhing in their rainy
dreams of guarding armor, gemstones and gold.

And those fallen boulders below, on the sand . . .
if we were to rest on those, we'd be at the end,
there'd be nothing left for us. (But the sunset
clouds glow jewel-fiery across the sinking sun.
Jewel-fiery . . . ) Or of us: nothing. Cold wet stone.

*−after Luis de Góngora (1623)*

24

# Spell

But this charm's green in the red world—
low leaf that opens anyway
among dry pebbles, by a hard road.
In the chained world, this charm is free.

A private charm against goodbyes
when you and I release each other—
the farewell kiss, these lost-child cries
we swallow, this turning to a feather.

I kiss your mouth. That's what I seek.
This charm's a statement and reply.
And a seed, a wedge, a way to take
what's good into our work today.

This kiss is given at the border of night.
Leaf that is ours, love that is green,
give us all more life, more blue-note
soul hours and days together again.

*–after Bertolt Brecht*

# Afterward

Across fields of native weeds holding their breath,
      and cows breathing,
we escaped as far as a stand of slow-fleeing trees.

Screaming more and more, the devoted, hardworking
      ambulances nearby began
rushing away toward ERs and then to gasoline bars.

We lay down on our frightened raincoats.
      Our shadows among the oaks
remained on tiptoe, on watch in all directions.

We lay there till in moonlit midnight came more
      assault-rifle shooting elsewhere.
The wind winged away gasping and hid in ditches

with the surviving children, the ditches
      dug themselves deeper into
clayey dread, and dark ravines crowded up into

our helpless thoughts, and memories of
      earlier times of such chaos
rushed through you. And then, deep into interior

rifts of the earth your innerness, too, fled.
      I followed, looking back.
Everyone's lungs were bleating like smoke alarms—

but softly. And we keep hearing a command
      to forget. But to forget
would mean not helping everyone survive.


                  *−after Yehuda Amichai*

## Bow Seven Times

Near the river

Beside the railway
weedy with burdock,
the summer platform
(*Stay Behind Line!*), a
bright yellow footstool
awaiting the next
train . . . Let's step onto
it then far beyond
these tracks to the deck
of that green tugboat
that's preemptively
heading upriver
against one-wayness;
another yellow
step flies us up to
the wing of that small
airplane overhead,
and from there we will
vault at an angle
to what no compass
shows, to indirect

dimensions we can
not know, yet we do.

~

APEX

The skull has evolved
all its forehead-breadth,
temple to Temple,
is amused by its
own sutures, features,
futures. Omniscient,
its cupola gleams,
it froths with ideas,
dreams of itself—a
chalice (by some, used
as such) beyond all
chalices, mother-
land of mother tongues,
father of godhood,
cap of happiness
and horror, a star-
thinking exemplar.

~

## RHYME

I sense by its im-
perceptible touch
that from the farthest
remove of the known
universe a dazed
ray too weak to be
seen is standing on
my closed rhyming eyes.

I hear the whisper
of the phonetic
attraction between
two blood-warm iron-ore
verbs, the palpable
pebbly sound of them.

~

OUR MORTAL CAP

The cranium dome
hangs from its own thread
of virtual pale
light, conceiving its
exercises of
inventiveness, its
associative
super- supremo-
conductivity,
its color wheel of
lucid and lulu,
its murk and murder,
worthy and woo-woo
heterodoxies,
its Zeno, its Zeus,
its Dante, its Te
Deums and freak shows,
frescoes, twine theory,
money, bread, bricks, wine,
sex, six-syllable
abstractions, axes,
and genetic in-

genuities of
custom—including
kisses, grammar, the
vertical graves of
men buried upside
down without their heads.

~

WINTER

To the futile sound
of midnight church bells,
out back someone is
rinsing her thoughts in
unfathomable
universal sky—
a cold faint glowing.
Stars glint in the frost
white as salt on the
blade of an old axe.
Like mica in soil.
There's ice in the mouth
of the rain barrel.

Smash the ice—the sky
shivers in water,
the basalty earth
where the barrel squats
becomes transparent
underfoot, and there
too are galaxies,
ghost-pale, silent in
the seven-thousand-
odd chambers of our
inhuman being.

~

AN END

In dusk-lit ways, spell
me, tell me, little
swallow—Tuscan or
Tang or from other
sorrow times—how with-
out feather or wing
I too can find for

myself a grave made
only of the air.

~

MANDELSHTAM'S BEES

"For your sweet joy, take
"from my cupped hands a
"little glittering
"of sun, a little
"honey—for this is
"what Persephone's
"own bees commanded.

"A boat can't cast off
"if it isn't moored.
"No one can hear a
"shadow that wears fur
"boots. We can't best our
"fear in this dark wood.

"Our kisses: these are
"all that we can save,

"velvety as bees—
"which die if they are
"exiled from the hive.

"They're murmuring in
"the translucent groves
"of night. The far wilds
"of mountain Greece are
"their native land. Their
"diet is time, lung-
"wort, pale meadowsweet.

"For joy, please!—take this
"pagan gift: this rude
"rustling necklace of
"bees that have died, for
"these had transmuted
"honey into sun."

*—after Osip Mandelshtam (1912-1921)*

# Triage

Along my hospitable hall
I hear tongues speaking in people—
a kind and suffering, jumbled
and scared, multilingual choral
improvisation. From my bed,
I hear the patients and healers
conversing in disheveled rooms,
up crowded corridors of more
beds, following diagonals
of waiting, resignation, not
knowing, perhaps recovery.
In the whole inmost ward of my
self, the beds are occupied by
slow-moving remembrances like
time-lapse flower novels. At night,
now, outside the closed windows with-
in me, and outside the clinic,
I see tiny stars glittering
at the bare twig-tips of dark, cold,
sleeping, winter lindens, maples—
each twinkling branch-end a midnight
candelabrum of the cosmos.

*—after Boris Pasternak (1956)*

# T W O

*Two millennia gone,*
*and in their unknown graves lost*
*poems are still singing.*

—after Richard Wright

# On Song

Forgetting (named Lethe)
               is hated
by Memory's daughters,
               the Muses.


Lethe is not to be
               loved! Not She.


For mortals, what sweet power
               there is in
song. What deepest heart. What
               delight that


can make bearable this
               narrow, short
winding stream of life.

*−Sophocles (5<sup>th</sup> century BCE)*

# Pieces of Ancient Life

He who makes the journey
      to one in power is
his slave, even if when
      he set out he was free


~


Battle loves to hunt men down


~


A pity—the flute for the dance has stopped


~


    His joy made
him float like wind-
      blown thistledown


~


Early this morning, before the farm
slaves were up, I was carrying in,

for the young goats, fresh tender branches
I'd broken off for them, and I saw

an army marching in from where the
cape reaches farthest into the sea.

~

And whip-bait, too, branded thugs, eaters-
of what-belongs-to-others

~

Head down they hang like songbirds in a net

~

A scorpion stands watch among the rocks
. . . .
The dog thistle spreads across all the fields
. . .
How heavy on everything
are the thick cloaking cobwebs
. . .

A man is only breath and shadow

~

He shrieked like a falcon
　　　swooping down on fresh meat

~

Down the steep hills a grazing
　　　antlered deer would come slowly

lifting its nose
　　　and the fine points

of its wide rack, easing
　　　itself down unnoticed

~

As in the pale top leaves
　　　of a tall aspen—
even if in nothing else—
　　　high up this morning

the air moves a little, flutters
        one feather

~

In the smoke from the bright
        altar-flames in their streets
float sweet foreign scents of
        myrrh they burn drop by drop

~

        Many are the things I envy in your life—
most of all that you've never been to any foreign land

~

Oh what happiness could you
        have that is greater than this:
after reaching land, to lie
        down under the eaves and hear
in your sleeping thoughts not the
        ocean but steady small rain

~

She went rushing along in a bright-colored coat

*—Sophocles (fragments, 5ᵗʰ century BCE)*

# Obscure Heralds Robed All in Black

Life pounds us very hard . . . I don't know. I don't know!
Blows that might have come from God Himself, in disgust.
The blood of all we've suffered for so long wells up fast
then terrified it sinks back down—into the soul . . . I don't know!

For some, not so many blows. But they come . . . They crack open,
they contort, the fiercest face; they gash and scar the strongest back.
Maybe what they are is the half-wild young horses of inhuman
Attilas. Or heralds Death sends us all robed in black.

Jolts that knock the Christs within one's soul into long dire
plummets from a nice little faith that's been blasphemed by fate.
Bloody blows!—They sound like the crackling, as we stand and wait,
of our holy bread in the old oven—but the bread catches fire!

Human beings! Poor things, poor things! This way and that, we look—
did somebody come up from behind and clap us on the back?
Wide-eyed, skittish, we stare—is this somehow our own fault?
Everything we've gone through sloshes like a foul puddle of guilt.

Life . . . hammers us . . . hard as stone . . . I don't know. I just don't know.

*–César Vallejo (1918)*

45

## Audacity & Apogee

I want to write but my mouth speaks only a foam.
Whatever I might utter, I'm stuck in word-mud.
No number I speak can matter except the sum total.
And no secret core means no written pyramid.

Yes, I want to write. But I'm only a mute beast.
Yes, I'd like a laurel wreath. But I stew like an onion.
There's no cough, well-worded or not, that isn't just mist.
There's no god or son of god except with evolution.

So let's get out of here!—and therefore eat grass
and roasted sobs. And our own meek souls, we'll eat,
pickled in brine, we'll swill black wine sweetened with aspartame.
Let's go! Let's go! I've tear-gassed
myself! Let's drink whatever we drank that last time.
(Come on, Crow—you numbskull—let's go hump your mate.)

*—César Vallejo (1937)*

# On Argyle Street

Smoky, cold, broken late-afternoon clouds
          mob eastward. Roaming west, I see on side-
walks no one I know, no one who knows me.
          Yet from all our wandering at this same
hour come shared underthoughts that we can sense.
          Then, again, that which is not darkness can
undarken our obscurity, justly
          slant from sky to make bleak ice meekly gleam.

*−after Wang Wei (8<sup>th</sup> century CE)*

# View from an Oklahoma Hilltop

The wind saws itself against the thick blades of red granite ridges.
Over the jagged boulder-humps and tumbled-down peaks
of these low stoop-shouldered former mountains it scrapes itself.
Its breath riffles the rainwater pools in shallow stone hollows.

The high rock ridge is splashed white with hawk-scat
and with a quartz-cracking lichen like cold yellow-orange flame.

Below, a harrier glides over the dry lake bed—
dead shells, savage little burrs, a delicate sharp-toothed skull.

The wind tears at itself and rushes
into voice through
spikey scrub-oak leaves.

The rattlesnake is wild.
The spider is wild.
The cougar is wild.

What makes such savage wildness seem tame
is memories of what men have done.

*–after Chang Ko-Chiu (c. 1300 CE)*

# Lesson

The public corpse was rotting on the branch
like hideous fruit that drooped toward its stem.
The result and proof of a dubious decree,
above the road it swayed like a pendulum.

Its shameless nakedness, its bulging tongue,
its shock of hair straight up like a rooster's comb—
it had the look of farce. A ragged gang
of boys, all jokes, stood grinning beside my horse.

And the mournful sack of guts, with its bowed head—
a bloated outrage on the short green tree
for hangings—vented its putrid stench in gusts
as in solemn censer arcs it swung. The sun
was climbing pulpit steps of flawless blue.
Landscapes like this, Tibullus put into song.

*–Salvador Díaz Mirón (1901)*

# Lurid and Lunatic

To such absurdity the daylight was deaf.
A seat in a minivan to some other place—
that's all I asked. All right, OK, I'll donate

more of my money to . . . the richest. No! OK!
No! At the inauguration I marched along
the edge of a ray of light that something
had bribed to a blur. An official bandit

demanded I never again vote. They said
I should sign. Sign it, they said. And why don't
those folks in the low-hope neighborhoods?
they said, They should buy our campaign hats, too,

it's dumb of them not to be nice, they don't
make sure to smile and cheer for the Big Guy,
and so he don't smile back. Well, I said, well . . .
eagle-eyed America cannot transit the eye

of no such needle. And then the bandit,
the tall one who'd stomped on my hopes
and blocked me getting on the citizen ship, he
began to cry into a red white and blue bucket,

hugging it, laughing with it, looking mean.
The huge crowd, huge, so huge, they'd got
soaked by the freezing tears of bruised clouds
shaped like alligators, and the petroleum-soggy

frauds of big real estate had spilled onto
the street and opioided the blind earth
under the aching feet of all the depressed trees
and the jackboots of the spokespersons for the Lost

Cause and Hell. And the daylight detested all
those limos that stood up on their hind wheels
and danced, and all the lurid and lunatic hoopla that
was staggering and howling and gurgling by.

*−after Marina Tsvetaeva (1918)*

## What Remains


Yes, bread that's poisoned. And not even one sip of air.
How hard it is for the wound of life to be cured.
Joseph himself, sold to Egypt as a slave,
could not have been more heavily grieved.

Then under the sky-swarm of stars, Bedouins come.
They quiet their horses. Then in turn, with eyes closed,
each invents some chanted fragment of their day
of epic nothing, that only brought them boredom,

for among such riders, little's needed to inspire—
in the dunes, one man lost a quiver of arrows,
others traded some geldings for a mare—events are
only a mist that thins and disappears.

But if—if—such songs are sung out to the end
with all the heart, with all the breath in the lungs,
almost everything vanishes . . . And what remains
is the desert vastness, the stars, the one who sings.

*—Osip Mandelshtam (1913)*

# Lips, Hands, Eyes

Lips that need no brand-names.

Hands that dream the score
of a gigue or await
an escape into fugues.

                    Eyes
that do not close when they see
hungry displaced children

or unpleasant paupers

or beat-up out-of-tune pianos

or books that are searching
a dim house for a lit lamp.

*—after Marina Tsvetaeva (1916)*

## Hyssop Garden on the Shore of Midnight

A crack zigzagged open in Time

In peeked Memory

~

Flowers opened in early morning
and shifting their hues till Night
crossed over Day

painting their Departure

~

My shadow
      so tired
      so thin

It wanted me to carry it on my back

~

           Our
           ravenous
           transitoriness

It's easy to hear it in the
       loneliness felt
       by each of our words


~


At the door—listen—

The silence when this day comes
       around again from
       its permanent ditch
       in History

   knocks
   at the door, so loud


~


   The evening
even though each day it digs
       its vast grave
       shoveled full of darkness

nevertheless emanates
into our sleep what we cannot
see when awake

~


Two wings beating
across the empty air from elm to copper beech
from laughter to weeping
                    from weeping to laughing

from musical keys
        to melodies
                    from harmonies


it's those singing wings on their
            way to dissonance

that beat the air
            for us, softly

~

Along the shore that's
the color
of feldgrau uniforms

a detour

                into mountains of the sky
                into orphans' colonies
                D.P. camps for rivers
                flames that burn black
                or white


~


Uttermost                           sand


~


faster, time


faster
when the second second
                    forces

the first to its knees
       out of breath, gasping in
       the hyssop garden
on the shore of midnight


*−after Nelly Sachs (1964)*

# Mirrors

*Into the front-hall mirror a cup of cocoa's*
*Evaporating, the window-curtains billow in and bang!—*
*Straight out the footpath to the orchard, into chaos*
*And toppled trees, this winged mirror rushes to the swing…*
                                   *—Boris Pasternak (1917)*


A round of thanks or
                     drinks for
my three best-loved books—
                     let's stand
them on their fleet or
                     swollen
stylistic feet for
                     photos:
with pen-feather arms
                     around
each other's inky
                     shoulders—
Hey, you outer two,
                     turn in
a little!—they hinge
                     themselves
into a front-hall

                    mirror
in a hushed household.
                    (Where is
everyone?) The e-
                    lixir
for which they thirst is
                    a cup
of that consciousness-
                    cocoa
in Pasternak's poem
                    that in
his Russian I can't
                    read and
in my English I
                    can't for-
get. His phrase for the
                    china
cup, his inflected
                    language,
still outlive wars, re-
                    volu-
tions, the tournaments
                    of grave-
diggers, ornaments

                    of verse,
anniversaries
                    of words
with hard lives and ach-
                    ing backs.
Three books—a three-winged
                    mirror
of mind canted at
                    angles
to catch whoever's
                    reading.
Let's praise their age and
                    pages.
That cup of cocoa
                    has flown
out the window and
                    down a
narrow path through thought
                    that's an
indigo shade. Mean-
                    while live-
ly trees elbow in-
                    to the
winged front-hall mirror

       and their
branches touch and break
         nothing.
A lantern by which
         something
has been written but
        isn't
finished . . . I see it
        outside
and inside, searching
        with its
one eye the elo-
        quent dusk.

# December Streetcar Ticket, 1920s Madrid

When the icy wind, that
      knows not how hard it blows,
how much it dismays us,
      incites the towers of
city lights against my
      being, you, my little
ticket, are the vivid
      new flower species whose
bright petals we see, we
      buy, in the planter-box
of the evening street-car . . .
      So briefly and bravely
fated, you rush us to
      the destinations that
you promise us, for on
      your petal a street name's
punched, and maybe, too, a
      connection. No, you're no
glowing Rose, and you say
      we need not Lament the
late (real) Miss Carnation.
      And yet there's a modern-
day model of a live
      flower—a violet,

I'd say—by which I mean:
     A book.  This too moves us
elsewhere—yes, even when
     it's tucked safely inside
a winter-coat pocket.

*–Rafael Alberti (1929)*

# The Names of Everyone

When my horse and I arrive
at the shattered past,
                          I spur her on.
But that lost, empty place
drags my spirit to itself, pulls me
                          away from me.
And as the mare quickens
her pace, the past keeps up with us—
                          leaping along
the rubble and tilted
stonework of half-fallen
                          walls and towers
and from tomb to tomb.
The mare's hooves clop softly
                          in the pale dirt
of winding narrow weed-field
paths where most of this gone
                          city once stood—
I'm not the only one who's tried
to go back beyond such wholly
                          emptied places.
Rocking-chair oak limbs are creaking
under the heavy dead souls
                          that perch on them.

Two extinct avian species that
I recognize offer their alarm
                    calls to this hour.
As the horse and I cross soft
shadowed ground underneath
                    a stand of pines,
another bird, some cautious thrush
I don't know the name of, catches
                    my mood, looking
me straight in the mind, its tiny
nearly weightless body angled
                    quizzically.
I ask my horse the bird's name. She
only glances at me, then says:
                    "Can you tell me—
What were the names of everyone
of whom now no one knows?"

                    *—after Hanshan (c. 800 CE)*

## Ambular y deambular

It turns out that I'm so tired of being a man. Parties
and dinners, I get there too early—wilted, wordless.
Yet the door I can't open is me.  I'm a plastic swan-
toy left for dead in a motel pool of ancestors and ashes.

The sight of crowded day-labor street corners makes me
cringe and wail. I just want some rest!—the way stones rest,
or bolts of wool. I want to not keep gawking with my left eye
at courthouses or violent street busts or little kids alone
on the sidewalks, or in pawn shops the eyeglasses and violins,
or at the hideously happy shouters at fascist rallies.

I'm tired of my own two feet. I'm tired, it so happens,
of my toenails, my hands, my shoulders, my shadow.
It turns out I'm so tired of being a man like me. So tired.

But . . . well, OK, but do I—on a lark—mock a nasty
county clerk or a senator with the gift of a bouquet
of stinking weeds? Or a priest I know—get a lawyer
for his victims? Yeah, it would be beautiful to stroll the sidewalk
swinging a long, sharp myth—green blade, green handle!—
and shouting . . . till the Chicago cold freezes me to death.

I don't want to be a root any more—me too, a twisty sociopath,
gloomy and shivering, pushing and pushing (what
else can I do?) my unconscious hand into the wet guts
of the earth to get whatever's down there. One blind root
pulling up another. Every day. Pondering it. Gnawing at it.

I can't atone for what I've done— it's all regrets and guilt and dread.
I don't want these bathetic setbacks of mine. I don't want
to exist as some freakish eyeless underground root
throwing up his tendril hands at everything that's wrongful
when I've gone through some beat-up alley door and down
basement stairs into a coffin-club jammed with the dancing dead.

That's why when Monday sees me coming it burns
like stolen gasoline. When it sees my jailhouse face it runs,
and then for twenty-four hours it shrieks like a wounded wheel
you could follow into the night by its bloody tracks.

Inside clammy depressions that I think you know, too, Mondays
shoulder me into the darkest corners. Mondays send me to clinics
where bones are jumping out the windows. Mondays shove me
into mostly empty bars reeking of toxins as well as booze.
Mondays fill the ERs with plague victims, each now alone.

Looking in through the window of an animal shelter
I can't endure those dog leashes dangling from a nail.
In half-asphyxiated trees, birds look the color of bile.
On café tables I've seen false teeth that people forgot.
Really, mirrors everywhere should be weeping with shame
and calling, "Help, please!" Crop tops . . . muscle shirts . . .
tweets . . . online creeps, pandemic parties in the streets!

So as calmly as I can, with my shoes on, with my hurts
on, with my eyes on, I walk and walk, I'm filled with feverish
diminutions and tarragon memories, I walk
and I wander—past prosthetics shops and comedy clubs,
past empty storefronts and sick sleeping beggars and sunless
dank cul-de-sacs where people's wire clotheslines sag and drip
polluted tears from socks and sheets and shirts.

*—after Pablo Neruda (1933-34)*

# On Sleep

Favor us, Lord Sleep! Sunrise
                radiance that reaches
everywhere—keep this from our
                eyes! And bring Yourself to
us instead! Come, we pray! Our
                Restorer! Our Healer!

Sleep, You that never suffer
                Pain! Sleep, knowing nothing
of torment or grief!—come rule
                over us, come breathing
sweetly, sweetly . . .

*–Sophocles (410 BCE)*

## Elderly Greek Scribe at a Temple
## of the Muses

Do you see him?—
     He's offering his little heavy discus of lead
     for marking the margins and the columns.
And his knife—for trimming and notching his reed pens.
And his straightest ruler.
And his dry, ink-stained, fine-pored pumice stone
     from the beach—for absorbing
     excess ink, and for gently
     rubbing away a wrong mark.
He places the four things there, together.

It's not silver, not gold—but it's his grateful
donation today in honor of the Muses.

Only everyday things—worth nothing.

Yes, of course. But old age has clouded his eyes.

He can't work any more. And these
are the only valuables he's ever owned.

        *—after Philippos of Thessaloniki (first century* CE)

## Discus

Discus—starred

                                        constellated

with prehistories


                        tellings

and foretellings


                                try

throwing yourself


                out


                                        of yourself.


                                        *–Paul Celan (1967)*

# T H R E E

*En la ardua vigilia de la lectura, cuando*
*la sangre se hace luz, pensamos que la flecha*
*podría atravesarnos sin herirnos.*

—Rosario Castellanos, "Los engañados"

(In the arduous wakefulness of reading, when
our blood becomes light, we think the arrow
might pass through us without wounding us.)

# My Greco-Russian Investigation
## (after Pindar's Third Pythian Ode)

Dear "Hieron" (I'll call you—not your made-  *strophe 1*
        up *lump* of a name),
A friend came from your tyrannical
        capital to tell
me you're ill in spirit and in mind.
        If it were no shame
to wish you some good, then I'd long for
        Kheiron, the centaur
son, long dead, of a goddess, to be
        alive among us
again—great four-legged lord of forests
        and mountain meadows
who foster-fathered that maker of
        remedies for harms,
ailments, disorders: Asklepios!—
        hero healer of
our maladies, our bloody wounds and
        blows of battle, strife
of spirit, the discord among kin,
        peoples, even thieves
like you. . . . But if he were here, could this
        great healer cure you?

As we know, Koronis before she      *antistrophe 1*
        birthed Asklepios,
was slain on her pillows by fletched shafts
        from the immortal
bow of Artemis—Apollo wished
        it so. The dead young
mother's blood-stained shade descended to
        Hades' house. . . . (Don't think,
Hieron, there's nothing that can check you!)
        The doomed mother-to-
be of the healer-to-be, in her
        fluttering ardor,
had thought little of (and had not told
        her father, horseman
Phleygus, of) her simple appetite
        for pleasure in her
soft fragrant bed with a lovely young
        man. . . . But—after she
had lain with the world-vigilant, far-
        seeing God of Song?!?!
(Hieron—might your own fat appetite
        be your fated end?)

And in her womb—Apollo's holy
        semen! His
excellence! All she'd wanted, before
        wedding Him,
was sweet revel. Lovely, she sought more
        loveliness.
Like you, she thought—this is only what
        I deserve.
But you build gilt towers to yourself!
        And you go
so low: you bend people's darkest hopes
        toward more
darkness, you whip them to follow you
        while you take
from them what they need, and what do you
        save for them?
Nothing. You mock, demean, demonize
        other poor
souls whom they fear. And you incite them
        to rampage.
You stir them to mob up in fury,
        lift torches.
You abandon the addicted and
        the sick, you

stick them with cutbacks, give your pals more
        profits, and
leave people weeping in a storm-ditch.

Koronis of the
        gorgeous raiments was at last
the victim of her
        illusions, her privilege,
and committed her
        folly, Hieron. (D'ya get that?)
And (just like you!) she
        was heard, seen!—by an ever-
surveilling power
        on watch in His high temple:
Apollo. . . . Even
        though amidst distracting gifts
brought to Him there—gold
        lyres, bows, bright arrows, tripods,
spears, rows of candles,
        and outside, fat flocks and herds,
He saw her!—His true
        informant was His own mind,
knowing all, sure of

all . . . mulling all. Apollo
does not lie, nor can
                    mortals deceive Him by word,
deed, fraud, hoax, hustle,
                    sting, scheme, flimflam, scam or sham.


Watchful Apollo's                                          *antistrophe 2*
                    mind deduced for Him the sight
of sweet Koronis
                    in bed with her illusion
of love, and showed Him
                    her naiveté, simple
heart, defenselessness. . . .
                    Even so, for Him His fierce
sister, Artemis,
                    flew to bring incandescent
revenge to the cheat,
                    Koronis, on His behalf—
to the quiet lake
                    house where Koronis thought she
was hidden—near the
                    same mountainsides that Kheiron
once had known and roamed!

                        The young woman's fate found and
annihilated
                        her and some close to her who
knew what she'd done but
                        saw her thoughtless transgression
as something one should
                        allow. But there's no stopping
a righteous spark that
                        sets fire to a green forest.

            Koronis' family                                    *epode 2*
            prepared her funeral.
            In one stride, Apollo
            stood beside her blazing
            pyre. The flames parted for
            His divinity. He
            seized and rescued His un-
            born infant son and flew
            to centaur Kheiron. To
            him He gave this child half-
            godly, to be taught to
            heal mortal afflictions:
            great Asklepios! (Your

deserved end, Hieron, is
now certain. In you, what
is there that could be healed?)

Everyone who went to the Healer                                   *strophe 3*
          bearing their
sores and cankers, their tumors and boils,
          battle wounds
from sharp bronze, pitiless arrows that
          had struck them
from afar, those whose bodies trembled
          with fevers
or chills, and others—all these, with spells,
          with chants, he
healed, he soothed. He administered his
          own potions,
he bandaged with balms the several
          parts of the
body, and on many he worked with
          hands and blade
to revive their limbs, rebuild their might.
          But Hieron,
listen: Even deep wisdom (such as

you don't have
and you despise), even sacred skill
      such as his—
can be in thrall to profit. Much gold
      was pressed on
Asklepios, unholying his
      healer's hands. . . .


So much gold. . . . And for even more, he          *antistrophe 3*
      did what he
alone among mortals could: he dared
      to devise
new miraculous ways on a dead
      man till this
man breathed again!—after Hades had
      hidden him
from all his mourners! . . . . Asklepios
      was handed
his gold. Instantly Zeus, the son of
      Kronos, with
one wave of his sovereign hand, took
      the breath from
both men's breasts and both fell dead—blasted

by Zeus's
lightning, too. . . . With our merely mortal
         minds, Hieron,
we must seek from justice—that is, from
         the nature
of the good—what is best for all, what
         is right for
all. You're covetously, hoggishly
         wrong. Take straight
steps, Hieron!—toward the well-being of
         your own mind.

If the centaur were still living in                          *epode 3*
his cave, and if I could have sung to
him some soothing soul-song, honey-sweet,
I might have persuaded him to teach
a new healer to cure the love of
riches and power which so fills you,
dreadful Hieron. To bring sanity
to you, I myself would have journeyed
far across the dark seas to you in
a fast ship, I'd have voyaged long sea-
roads to the monuments of human-

kind demeaned by your pyrite towers,
your rivers of unclean currency
into which you've lowered your double
gold-plated goblet so many times.
You with your dead, gold-dyed hair; the fake
gold beard of your soul, your fool's-gold face!
Your fixers, pols, cronies and toadies!
Mendacious evasions; invasive
avarice; heedless treason—aren't these
the coming doom of your mulish peeves,
your bluffs, your bullshit, your underworld
gambles, your shell-within-shell-game fraud?

Civil to citizens and to all                                    *strophe 4*
        river gods, mountain gods,
all cities, plains, coasts, you should be. But
        no, you will not. You won't!
Fields, farms and towns are vulnerable.
        Cities should be cherished
as sanctuaries—and the broad plains,
        hill-heights and harbors where
they stand. The places we all have not
        despoiled still breathe themselves

into our spirits. Begrudge nature
        when we so need it? Why
assault your own nation? If I could
        make a safe journey, I'd
bring you blessings—for your people's health
        and for the full, quick de-
contamination of your soul. But
        my blessings cannot re-
deem your destructiveness—your hatred,
        callousness, vengefulness.
You swindle humanity itself.
        You borrow to rule, and
your cash and existential debts stink
        everywhere. Even if
you atoned for your worst deeds and words,
        none will ever admire
even the least of your evils but
        those who joined you in them.


I pray and hope only for you to                    *antistrophe 4*
        fall. May the mother of
all the gods—that goddess who Herself
        is the mothering Earth
whom you abuse, demean, endanger,

as a woman—may She,
our great and only home, hear, in peace-
ful night the singing of
Pan and girls and boys, in quiet streets,
who chant and choir to Her—
to console Her, praise Her, thank Her, and
revere and pray for Her
under the stars. (As you, Hieron, do
not. And near you, children
can't risk chorusing—you bode obscene
pained ruin for children.)
Both ancient sayings and new knowledge
speak to us, and you should
attend what good souls, old and new, have
taught us: our own fate is
measured out to us in gains and in
losses. Fools, cheats, knaves don't
bear this truth with grace. Good persons do
try to bear it—giving
to others, honoring the good in
others, bringing succor
to—not suckering—the sick, harassed,
poor, shunned, hurt, and oppressed.

If anyone's to be respected and admired,                    *epode 4*
               it is one
who rules well and without chasing after his own
               spoils and cons.
Let's consider heroic Kadmos, so unlike
               you or the
utterly unheroic people around you
               who expect
rewards, not the prosecution and shame they'll get.
               To Kadmos
came dreadful, heart-freezing trouble, yet he earned his
               immortal
blessings (while to Nixion came full disaster—
               as to you
it's coming. . . ). In Thebes, Kadmos's ecstatic joy
               surpassed all
his power of imagining when he wedded
               the dark-eyed,
divine, exquisite Harmonía, and this god-
               like man was
even allowed to hear the songs of Apollo's
               mountain-throned,
holy, teleo-perfect, inspiring Muses,
               crowned with light. . . .

They sang at the wedding feast, as          *strophe 5*
        dragon-slaying Kadmos
gazed at the immortal offspring
        of Kronos on their gold
dais, and their flawless hands gave
        him the bounty of their
glorious Olympian gifts. . . .
        But in later times came
anguish for this groom and bride—their
        three living daughters stole
the parents' joy by giving grave
        offense to the fierce god
Dionysos, who punished them
        all with horrifying
reversals, remorse, grief. In His
        rage He transformed Kadmos
and Harmonía into snakes. . . .
        Years later, the divine
pity of Zeus restored their fair
        bodies. He made them death-
less, blessed. But no restoration
        can come, Hieron, to you.

Now you live in auto-inflamed
        blithering and TV.
Nixion—a devious man,
        like you—willfully schemed,
flouted laws, and set out to smash
        his "enemies" with his
power. Hot-tongued, brazen liar,
        egging on white race-hate—
Nixion was, however, far
        more patriotic than
you and your malevolent pals.
        When you shrug, you blight. You
wreck. You corrupt. You laze. You'll sell
        out anyone, any-
thing. You slither away yet you
        can't help leaping back to
your crimes, slurs, and whining. You sneer,
        jeer, deny, belittle,
you destroy the state, you hide bribes
        inside frauds inside thefts. . . .
(Zeus bound Nixion on a fire-
        wheel spinning forever.)

Forever your name will be a sump
        of greed and lust,
        treason for
gain, of dodges, rackets, and fixes,
        and your counter-
        feit soul. Your
colossal ignorance, your monstrous
        oblivion
        and disdain,
your arrant lack of compassion, your
        glacial soul. Your
        infantile
petulance. And among others, I
        will be one
        who tells of the
ancient style of your villainous spite,
        pique, casual
        cahoots, self-
dealing in pelf and transgressions, your
        avid and
        inveterate
billionizing (your heavy purse seems
        testicular
        to you). Your

will thrashes about, you're starved for self-
    abasing
    cowed praise from your
courtiers. (In private they hate your
    blunders and
    gluttonous guts.)
We abhor your exulting in sad-
    istic dis-
    avowals, gro-
tesque deceit, racial despisals, con-
    tempt for the
    weak.  You're by far
the maximum absurdist ever
    to choke on
    the corrosive
gall of your own vile blabbermouthing.


In these terrible times of small good,
    I become
    small. In times of
greatness, I do not become great. But
    with skills of
    mind and mother-

tongue I will honor whatever fair
>fortune is
>given to me
and mine. If I am to win any
>reward, may
>it be a mite
of fame, having practiced how to frame
>with wordman-
>ship dispraises
and praises, which I write and recite.
>Honest phrase-
>craft and a true
ear help hold our heroes close, for their
>long, large-souled
>devotion to
just and generous purposes. In
>long-ago
>times, verses turned
by adroit song-makers were for an
>admiring
>good remembrance.
May I, even if only with what
>I write, be
>an ally, in

my verses, for an ally, but the
      foe of my
      foe—a wolf to
chase and chase him down. No matter what
      path he takes,
      I will follow.


*−the original was composed by Pindar between 478 and 467 BCE*

One's work and life as a writer are built on a deep dependency on other writers. Because poetry is a longitudinal artistic study of human existence, our existential and poetic sources extend from contemporary back to ancient. This collection of versions of, riffs on, and responses to poems in several languages is intended as an honoring of particular poets and poems. They have led me, over years of the practice of poetry, to turns and possibilities of poetic thinking and feeling and crafting that I would not have been able to discover alone.

My "renditions" are not only covers, versions, borrowings and thefts, but also, I hope—after having brought poems or specific lines out of their linguistic and cultural home and into ours—at least a small restitution for the translator's initial infraction of rendering (that is, transporting the original poem to the realm of a different language). One can try to show one's fellow English-language readers subtle resources of poetry, and of textures of our language, that the original poem can infuse into English. Osip Mandelshtam wrote (1932), "I want to go outside our language / because of everything that ties me to it forever." One can also try to express poetic gratitude to a few of the great dead.

Many of these poems are "after" (or developed from) an original poem or only a few lines of that poem; I absorb a poetic energy that carries me toward my own compositional opening. Other poems closely track—in the sense of following a trail through a forest of symbols and word-sounds—the original poem. Sometimes I'm more interested in following the poetic thinking of the original poem than the meanings of particular words, because poetic thinking can move like montage, creating meaning by contrasts and in gaps. A poem is not a word list; it's a choreography of feeling, perception, and thought. And the Muse is within the poet and also in poems themselves.

Sources (in the order of the poems):

On the section title pages, the haikus by Richard Wright (#7 and #152) are from *Haiku: The Last Poems of an American Icon*, edited by Yoshinobu Hakutani and Robert L. Tener, New York: Arcade, 2012. The lines by Rosario Castellanos are from a poem in her complete poems, *Poesía no eres tú: Obra poética* (1948-1971), Mexico D.F., Fondo de Cultura Económica, 2004.

"Swear—": from the sense of song in three lines of Marina Tsvetaeva, Nov. 9, 1918, "I sing for God, not for people! / Songs are sung the way the heart beats— / It's alive—song is," as translated from Russian into French by Véronique Lossky, in *Poesie Lyrique: Poèmes de Russie (1912-1920)*, Paris: Editions Syrtes, 2015.

"Honeycombs and Cobwebs": after Osip Mandelshtam (1891 – 1938), poem 108 in *Collected Works (Sobranie Sochineny)*, vol. 1, revised and expanded edition, 1967. "Your name" may mean the name of God.

"Anemone": after lines by Boris Pasternak (1890 – 1960) in three poems of his *My Sister—Life*, (composed 1917, published 1922), as translated from Russian by Ilya Kutik and Reginald Gibbons from Boris Pasternak, *Sobranie Sochineny v 4 tomakh (Collected Works in Four Volumes)*, Moscow, Khudozhestvennaya Literatura, 1989.

"Boy, Hiding": after Eugenio Montale (1896 – 1981), "Meriggiare pallido e assorto" (1916; 1922), in *Ossi di Seppia* (1925).

"Paris . . . Moscow, 1925": after lines in two poems of Marina Tsvetaeva (1892 –1941) addressed to Boris Pasternak, dated March 24 (*"Des versts, des miles, des dis-tances"*) and May 7, 1925 (*"Bonjour de ma part au siegle russe"*), as translated from Russian into French by Véronique Lossky, in *Poesie Lyrique: Poèmes de maturité (1921-1941)*, Paris: Editions Syrtes, 2015.

"The God Eros, Who Cannot Be Thwarted": Sophocles (c. 497/6 – winter 406/5 BCE), fragment 684, from his lost play *Phaedra*, Loeb Classical Library vol. 483.

"One Leaf, Two Leaves": after Luis Cernuda (1902-1963), "Como leve sonido," in his 1931 book, *Los placeres prohibidos* (*Forbidden Pleasures*), included in his complete poems, *La realidad y el deseo*, Mexico: Fondo de Cultural Económica, 1970.

"But What Does He Do?": after Luis Cernuda (1902-1963), "Desdicha," in his 1929 collection, *Un río, un amor* (*A River, A Love*), in *La realidad y el deseo*, Mexico: Fondo de Cultura Económica, 1970.

"But a Guy Goes By": after César Vallejo (1892 – 1938), "Un hombre pasa," in *Poemas Póstumos*, in *Obra Poética, Edición Crítica*, Madrid: Collección Archivos, 1988.

"Elegy: Green We Love You Green": after lines of Federico García Lorca's *"Romance Sonámbulo,"* in his 1928 book *Romancero Gitano*.

"Back to the Village": a translation of César Vallejo (1892 – 1938), from *Trilce* (LXI), in *Obra Poética, Edición Crítica*, Madrid: Collección Archivos, 1988.

"On the Continent's Far Edge": after a sonnet by Luis de Góngora (1561-1627), "Infiere, de los achaques de la vejez . . ."

"Spell": after Bertolt Brecht (1898 – 1956) Many years ago I copied into a notebook a few lines of Brecht in German, from which this poem grew. But I never again could find that poem by Brecht.

"Afterward": after Yehuda Amichai (1924-2000). A decade or so ago I made a version of this poem from a trot of the Hebrew original that was provided to me by a student, but I have lost the biobliographical information I would have put here, and now have only a word-for-word translation of the title, "Afterward, Among the Olive Trees." I have been unable to find the poem in any anthology of translations of Amichai's work that I have consulted.

"Bow Seven Times": after lines by Osip Mandelshtam (1891 – 1938) in several poems (nos. 92, 113, 126, 135, 227, 352, 362), and my translation of the complete poem 116 (composed 1920) in *Collected Works* (*Sobranie Sochineny*), vol. 1, revised and expanded edition, 1967.

"Triage": after a few lines in Boris Pasternak, "In the Hospital" (1956), as translated by Ilya Kutik and Reginald Gibbons, from Boris Pasternak, *Sobranie Sochineny v 4 tomakh* (*Collected Works in Four Volumes*), Moscow, Khudozhestvennaya Literatura, 1989.

"On Song": Sophocles (c. 497/6 – winter 406/5 BCE), fragment 568, Loeb Classical Library vol. 483.

"Pieces of Ancient Life": Sophocles (c. 497/6 – winter 406/5 BCE), Fragments 873, 554, 828f, 868, 434, 329, 431, 37, 767, 718, 286, 13, 89, 23, 840, 584, 636, 586, Loeb Classical Library, vol. 483.

"Obscure Heralds Robed All in Black": César Vallejo (1892 – 1938), "Los heraldos negros" is the title poem of his first book, included in *Obra Poética, Edición Crítica*, Madrid: Collección Archivos, 1988.

"Audacity & Apogee": after César Vallejo (1892 – 1938), "Intensidad y altura," in *Poemas Póstumos*, in *Obra Poética, Edición Crítica*, Madrid: Collección Archivos, 1988.

"On Argyle Street": after Wang Wei (c. 700-761 CE), "Deer Park," available in many English translations, including Eliot Weinberger, *19 Ways of Looking at Wang Wei*, New York: New Directions, 2016.

"View from an Oklahoma Hilltop": after Chang Ko-Chiu (i.e. Zhang Keiju, 1270- 1348), a Sanqu poet of the Yuan dynasty.

"Lesson": Salvador Díaz Mirón (1983-1928), "Ejemplo," in *Poesías Completas*, Mexico DF: UNAM, 1941; originally published in his volume *Lascas* (Jalapa, 1901).

"Lurid and Lunatic": Marina Tsevetaeva (1892 – 1941), after a French translation by Véronique Lossky of an untitled poem dated 27 July 1918, beginning "*Ma journée est absurd non-sens,*" in Marina Tsvetaeva, *Poesie Lyrique (1912-1941)*, vol. I, "Poèmes de Russie (1912-1920)," Editions Syrtes, 2015.

"What Remains": Osip Mandelshtam (1891 – 1938), poem 54 in *Collected Works (Sobranie Sochineny)*, vol. 1, revised and expanded edition, 1967.

"Lips, Hands, Eyes": after lines by Marina Tsvetaeva (1892 – 1941) in a poem dated July 2, 1916, beginning "*Les mains me sont données…,*" translated from Russian into French by Véronique Lossky, in *Poesie Lyrique (1912-1941)*, Vol. I, "*Poèmes de Russie (1912-1920),*" Paris: Editions Syrtes, 2015.

"Hyssop Garden on the Shore of Midnight": after Nelly Sachs (1891-1970), passages from *Glühende Rätsel* (*Glowing Enigmas*) (bilingual edition), translated by Michael Hamburger, Portland: Tavern Books, 2013.

"Mirrors": from four lines of Boris Pasternak's "Mirror" in *My Sister—Life* (composed 1917, published 1922), as translated from Russian by Ilya Kutik and Reginald Gibbons from Boris Pasternak, *Sobranie Sochineny v 4 tomakh* (*Collected Works in Four Volumes*), Moscow, Khudozhestvennaya Literatura, 1989.

"December Streetcar Ticket, 1920s Madrid": after Rafael Alberti (1902 – 1999), from *Cal y canto*, 1929.

"The Names of Everyone": Hanshan ("Cold Mountain"; ninth century CE). My version draws on several different translations into English, including Gary Snyder's in *Riprap and Cold Mountain Poems* (1958; 1959; 2009).

"Ambular y deambular": after Pablo Neruda (1904 – 1973), "Walking Around," in *Residencia en la tierra*, part 2, in *Obras Completas I, De "Crepusculario" a "Las uvas y el viento" 1923-1954*, Barcelona: Galaxia Gutenberg, 1999.

"On Sleep": after Sophocles (c. 497/6 – winter 406/5 BCE), *Philoktetes*, lines 828-32, Loeb Classical Library, vol. 21.

"Elderly Scribe at a Temple of the Muses": Philippos of Thessaloniki (first century CE), Loeb Classical Library, *Greek Anthology* 6.62.

"Discus": Paul Celan (1920 – 1970), "Wurfscheibe, mit," *Gedichte* vol. 2, Frankfurt: Suhrkamp Verlag, 1975; originally published in the posthumous 1970 volume, *Lichtzwang*.

"My Greco-Russian Investigation (Pindar's Third Pythian Ode)": a complete version, formally exacting—even if inadequately so in comparison with the ancient Greek ode (Loeb Classical Library, vol. 56), which I have adapted to the world-rattling and catastrophic American year 2017. (This poem was written between Jan. 17 and July 4, 2017.) Pindar's ode was composed sometime between 476 and 467 BCE. Hieron had earlier commissioned Pindar to write a victory ode for his winning chariot team and driver at the Olympian games of 468 (Pindar's First Olympian Ode); he was the *tyrannos*—king, tyrant, potentate—of Syracuse in Sicily from 478 to 467. His teams and drivers won several such races at the annual Greek games. This Third Pythian Ode was grouped by ancient editors with Pindar's surviving odes to victors in one sport or another at the games in Delphi. But this particular song-poem was written as a get-well wish. Unlike the tone of voice of my poem, regarding the ruler whom I address, Pindar's tone in this ode to his patron Hieron is solicitous regarding the ruler's declining health. Yet Pindar also does offer Hieron advice about ruling; we can infer that such advice was at least a gentle reprimand, even if Pindar's ode is of course flattering. (Pindar no doubt hoped to receive another commission from Hieron.) No leeway for flattery offered itself in my version. "Hieron died in 466/5 in Aetna and was given the honours of a hero there [ . . . ]. By contrast with the popular Gelon he was regarded as a despotic and repressive ruler" (*Brill's New Pauly* encyclopedia). Of course, unlike the ancient Hieron, my modern one, in order to gain power over his deceived "homeland" (*Heimat*, he might wish to call it), solicited and welcomed the aid of criminals and another tyrant. A footnote: in Pindar's ode, his Nixion (an obscure figure in Greek mythology), was, like ours (a prominent figure in the annals of political corruption), punished for transgressions—Nixion's, heedlessly amorous; Nixon's, crooked, knavish, amoral.

I thank the editors of the following magazines for publishing some of the poems in this collection (a number of them in earlier versions): *A Public Space, At Length, Fifth Wednesday, LitHub, On the Sea Wall*, and *Plume Poetry 9*. Many other poems in this collection were first published as translations (rather than "renditions") in several volumes (some of these also in earlier versions): Luis Cernuda, *Selected Poems*; Sophocles, *Selected Poems: Odes and Fragments*. Other "renditions" were first published (in earlier versions) in my books *Roofs Voices Roads, Saints, Maybe It Was So, Sparrow: New and Selected Poems, Slow Trains Overhead*, and *Last Lake*.

Reginald Gibbons is the author of eleven poetry collections. His *Creatures of a Day* was a finalist for the National Book Award. His book *Saints* won publication in the National Poetry Series. Volumes of his selected poems in translation have been published in Spain (*Desde una barca de papel*), Italy (*L'Abitino Blu*) and France (*Je pas je*). His novel *Sweetbitter* won the Anisfield-Wolf Book Award, and he has also published a book of very short fiction, *An Orchard in the Street*. Gibbons is the author of a book on poetic technique, *How Poems Think*. He has won fellowships from the Guggenheim Foundation, the National Endowment for the Arts, and the Center for Hellenic Studies, as well as the Folger Library's O. B. Hardison, Jr. prize and other honors and awards. His work has been included in the *Best American Poetry* and Pushcart Prize anthologies. He teaches at Northwestern University, where he is a Frances Hooper Professor of Arts and Humanities.

Gibbons' translations of poetry include Sophocles, *Selected Poems: Odes and Fragments*; Luis Cernuda, *Selected Poems*; and volumes in progress of selected poems of Boris Pasternak and of Marina Tsvetaeva, co-translated with Ilya Kutik. With Charles Segal, Gibbons co-translated Sophocles' *Antigone* and Euripides' *Bakkhai*; with Anthony L. Geist, he co-translated Jorge Guillén, *The Poetry and the Poet*. His edited volumes include *The Poet's Work*, *The Writer in Our World*, and *New Writing from Mexico* (for which he translated the work of 27 poets). His co-edited books also include *From South Africa: New Writing, Photography and Art* (with Jane Taylor, David Bunn and Sterling Plumpp) and Thomas McGrath, *Life and the Poem* (with Terrence Des Pres). Gibbons has edited four works by William Goyen, including the posthumous volume, *Had I A Hundred Mouths: New & Selected Stories, 1947-1983*; the 50th-anniversary edition of *The House of Breath*; the posthumous novel *Half a Look of Cain*; and Goyen's *Autobiographical Essays, Notebooks, Evocations, Interviews*.

Publication of this book was made possible by grants and donations. We are also grateful to those individuals who participated in our 2020 Build a Book Program. They are:

Anonymous (14), Robert Abrams, Nancy Allen, Maggie Anderson, Sally Ball, Matt Bell, Laurel Blossom, Adam Bohannon, Lee Briccetti, Therese Broderick, Jane Martha Brox, Christopher Bursk, Liam Callanan, Anthony Cappo, Carla & Steven Carlson, Paul & Brandy Carlson, Renee Carlson, Cyrus Cassells, Robin Rosen Chang, Jaye Chen, Edward W. Clark, Andrea Cohen, Ellen Cosgrove, Peter Coyote,  Janet S. Crossen, Kim & David Daniels, Brian Komei Dempster, Matthew DeNichilo, Carl Dennis, Patrick Donnelly, Charles Douthat, Morgan Driscoll, Lynn Emanuel, Monica Ferrell, Elliot Figman, Laura Fjeld, Michael Foran, Jennifer Franklin, Sarah Freligh, Helen Fremont & Donna Thagard, Reginald Gibbons, Jean & Jay Glassman, Ginny Gordon, Lauri Grossman, Naomi Guttman & Jonathan Mead, Mark Halliday, Beth Harrison, Jeffrey Harrison, Page Hill Starzinger, Deming Holleran, Joan Houlihan, Thomas & Autumn Howard, Elizabeth Jackson, Christopher Johanson, Voki Kalfayan, Maeve Kinkead, David Lee, Jen Levitt, Howard Levy, Owen Lewis, Jennifer Litt, Sara London & Dean Albarelli, David Long, James Longenbach, Excelsior Love, Ralph & Mary Ann Lowen, Jacquelyn Malone, Donna Masini, Catherine McArthur, Nathan McClain, Richard McCormick, Victoria McCoy, Ellen McCulloch-Lovell, Judith McGrath, Debbie & Steve Modzelewski, Rajiv Mohabir, James T. F. Moore, Beth Morris, John Murillo & Nicole Sealey, Michael & Nancy Murphy, Maria Nazos, Kimberly Nunes, Bill O'Brien, Susan Okie & Walter Weiss, Rebecca Okrent, Sam Perkins, Megan Pinto, Kyle Potvin, Glen Pourciau, Kevin Prufer, Barbara Ras, Victoria Redel, Martha Rhodes, Paula Rhodes, Paula Ristuccia, George & Nancy Rosenfeld, M. L. Samios, Peter & Jill Schireson, Rob Schlegel, Roni & Richard Schotter, Jane Scovell, Andrew Seligsohn & Martina Anderson, James & Nancy Shalek, Soraya Shalforoosh, Peggy Shinner, Dara-Lyn Shrager, Joan Silber, Emily Sinclair, James Snyder & Krista Fragos, Alice St. Claire-Long,

Megan Staffel, Bonnie Stetson, Yerra Sugarman, Dorothy Tapper Goldman, Marjorie & Lew Tesser, Earl Teteak, Parker & Phyllis Towle, Pauline Uchmanowicz, Rosalynde Vas Dias, Connie Voisine, Valerie Wallace, Doris Warriner, Ellen Doré Watson, Martha Webster & Robert Fuentes, Calvin Wei, Bill Wenthe, Allison Benis White, Michelle Whittaker, and Ira Zapin.